HADOOP

The Engine That Drives Big Data

By

Lars Nielsen

A New Street Executive Summary

2013

New Street Communications, LLC

Wickford, Rhode Island

newstreetcommunications.com

New Street Communications, LLC

Wickford, Rhode Island

newstreetcommunications.com

Contents

hadoop

Introduction

A leading programmer and systems administrator with more than 30 years experience, Lars Nielsen here provides an incisive yet user-friendly introduction to Hadoop – that most vital of tools for harvesting and sorting massive amounts of streaming, real-time, unstructured information and quickly gaining actionable Business Intelligence via Big Data Analytics. This report constitutes a detailed, 7,000-word executive-summary for those who need a fundamental understanding of Hadoop as a platform in order to fully grasp the complete depth and breadth of the mushrooming Big Data industry.

Writing for *InformationWeek,* Doug Henschen tells us: "Excitement around Hadoop has been building since its release as an open source distributed data processing platform [several] years ago. [The platform] has taken off, gaining customers, commercial support options, and dozens of integrations from database and data-integration software vendors. The top three commercial database suppliers – Oracle, IBM, and Microsoft – have adopted Hadoop. ... Will Hadoop turn out to be as significant as SQL, introduced more than 30 years ago? Hadoop is often tagged as a technology exclusively for unstructured data. By combining scalability, flexibility, and low cost, it has become the default choice for Web giants like AOL and ComScore that are dealing with large-scale clickstream analysis and ad targeting scenarios."

Hadoop is, quite simply, all over the place. Facebook, Yelp, Etsy, eBay and Salesforce are just a few of the franchises which use Hadoop as their key tool for harvesting, cleaning, digesting and analyzing the massive flood of data generated by their millions of customers and users every minute of every day.

Henschen continues: "Hadoop is headed for [even] wider use. It's applicable for all types of data and destined to go beyond clickstream and sentiment analysis. For example, SunGard, a hosting and application service provider for small and midsize companies, plans to introduce a cloud-based managed service aimed at helping financial services companies experiment with Hadoop-based MapReduce processing. And software-as-a-service startup Tidemark recently introduced a cloud-based performance management application that will use MapReduce to bring mixed data sources into product and financial planning scenarios."

The IDC conservatively predicts that Hadoop will represent a software market of approximately $816 million by 2016 while at the same time providing the bedrock solution for the Big Data market, which is in turn expected to become $23 BILLION dollar business by 2016.

The New Street Executive Summary you are about to read has been carefully-crafted to deliver a concise, user-friendly, jargon-free introduction to the Hadoop platform, carefully explaining both its strengths and its limitations as well as the fundamentals of how it works, how it evolved and why it is so vital to the future of BI.

Edward Renehan

Managing Director

New Street Communications, LLC

Wickford, RI

Listening to the data is important. … but so is experience and intuition. After all, what is intuition at its best but large amounts of data of all kinds filtered through a human brain rather than a math model?

- Steve Lohr

Big Data and Data Science Defined

The streets are abuzz with the terms "Big Data" and especially "Data Science," the late-breaking skill-set currently being deployed to harvest and interpret Big Data in order to gain actionable Business Intelligence (BI). The rapid emergence of elegant tools, paradigms and approaches for mining and querying Big Data is being hailed - rightly - as a business revolution as large as the first adoption of computers or, before that, the invention of the assembly line.

But while Information Technologists and tech-savvy venture capitalists shout from the rooftops, a vast array of entrepreneurs, investors, and managers find themselves caught somewhere in between the jargon and the reality. What exactly is Big Data? How can we get at it? Why is interpretation of Big Data so vital to today's businesses and, more importantly, those of tomorrow? And how does Hadoop - the much-touted "Holy of Holies" among Big Data tools - fit into the equation?

So, first of all, a few definitions.

"Big Data means extremely scalable analytics," Forrester Research analyst James Kobielus tells *Information Age*. "It means analyzing petabytes of structured and unstructured data at high velocity. That's what everybody's talking about."

As a catch-all term, Big Data is pretty nebulous. As *ZDNet's* Dan Kusnetzky notes: "If one sits through the presentations from ten suppliers of technology, fifteen or so different definitions are likely to come forward. Each definition, of course, tends to support the need for that supplier's products and services. Imagine that."

Industry politics aside, here's an unbiased definition of this complex field:

Every day of the week, we create 2.5 quintillion bytes of data. This data comes from everywhere: from sensors used to gather climate information, posts to social media sites, digital pictures and videos posted online, transaction records of online purchases, and from cell phone GPS signals – to name a few. In the 11 years between 2009 and 2020, the size of the "Digital Universe" will increase 44 fold. That's a 41% increase in capacity every year. In addition, only 5% of this data being created is structured and the remaining 95% is largely unstructured, or at best semi-structured. This is Big Data.

Per a recent analysis from IBM, Big Data Big comprises three dimensions: Variety, Velocity and Volume.

re: **Variety** – Big Data extends well beyond structured data, including unstructured data of all varieties: text, audio, video, click streams, log files and more.

re: **Velocity** – Frequently time-sensitive, Big Data *must be used simultaneously* with its stream in to the enterprise in order to maximize its value.

re: **Volume** – Big Data comes in one size: enormous. By definition, enterprises are awash with it, easily amassing terabytes and even petabytes of information. This volume presents the most immediate hurdle for conventional IT structures. It calls for scalable storage, and a distributed approach to querying. Many companies currently hold large amounts of archived data, but not the tools to process it.

(Note: To these, IBM's Michael Schroeck adds **Veracity**. In other words, a firm's imperative to screen out spam and other data that is not useful for making business decisions.)

Per Edd Dumbill (and no, that is not a typo), program chair for the O'Reilly Strata Conference and the O'Reilly Open Source Convention, Big Data "is data that exceeds the processing capacity of conventional database systems. The data is too big, moves too fast, or doesn't fit the strictures of your database architectures. To gain value from this data, you must choose an alternative way to process it."

Dumbill continues: "The hot IT buzzword … *Big Data* has become viable as cost-effective approaches have emerged to tame the volume, velocity and variability of massive data. Within this data lie valuable patterns and information, previously hidden because of the amount of work required to extract them. To leading corporations, such as Walmart or Google, this power has been in reach for some time, but at fantastic cost. Today's commodity hardware, cloud architectures and open source software bring Big Data processing into the reach of the less well-resourced. Big Data processing is eminently feasible for even the small garage startups, who can cheaply rent server time in the cloud."

Dumbill further explains that the value of Big Data falls into two categories: analytical use, and enabling new products. "Big Data analytics can reveal insights hidden previously by data too costly to process, such as peer influence among customers, revealed by analyzing shoppers' transactions, social and geographical data. Being able to process every item of data in reasonable time removes the troublesome need for sampling and promotes an investigative approach to data, in contrast to the somewhat static nature of running predetermined reports."

Overall, Big Data is – in its raw form – utter chaos. Approximately 80% of the effort involved in dealing with this largely-unstructured data is simply cleaning it up. Per Pete Warden in his *Big Data Glossary*: "I probably spend more time turning messy source data into something usable than I do on the rest of the data analysis process combined."

The Data Scientist takes the "chaos" of "messy source data" and finds within this morass the pure gold of actionable market information, and he or she uses Hadoop to do it.

If Hadoop is the "holy of holies" in the new religion of capturing and analyzing real-time transactional information, data scientists are most certainly the cult's "high priests and priestesses."

Data Science is a multidisciplinary endeavor combining a range of skills in a variety of fields, together with *a strong talent for creative, intuitive thinking: the envisioning of new and useful data sets.*

"I think of Data Science as a flag that was planted at the intersection of several different disciplines that have not always existed in the same place," says Hilary Mason, chief data scientist at bitly. "Statistics, computer science, domain expertise, and what I usually call 'hacking,' though I don't mean the 'evil' kind of hacking. I mean the ability to take all those statistics and computer science, mash them together and actually make something work."

Mason divides Data Science into two equally important functions. One half is analytics or, as she describes it, "counting things." The other half is the invention of new techniques that can draw insights from data that were not possible before. "Data Science is the combination of analytics and the development of new algorithms. You may have to invent something, but it's okay if you can answer a question just by counting. The key is making the effort to ask the questions. ... If I ask a question like 'how many clicks did this link get?' which is something we look at all the time, that's not a data science question. It's an analytics question. If I ask a question like, 'based on the previous history of links on this publisher's site, can I predict how many people from France will read this in the next three hours?,' that's more of a Data Science question."

"[Data Science] absolutely gives us a competitive advantage if we can better understand what people care about and better use the data we have to create more relevant experiences," says Aaron Batalion, chief technology officer for online shopping service LivingSocial, which uses technologies such as the Apache Hadoop data processing platform (to be discussed in a later chapter) to mine insights about customer preferences. "The days are over when you build a product once and it just works," Batalion comments. "You have to take ideas, test them, iterate them, [and] use data and analytics to understand what works and what doesn't in order to be successful. And that's how we use our big data infrastructure."

But without Hadoop, the Data Scientist is lost.

[Note: Portions of the previous chapter are drawn from my far more extensive coverage of Big Data and Data Science to be found in my book *A Simple Introduction to Data Science,* co-written with Noreen Burlingame.]

Hadoop Fundamentals

What lies at the heart of Big Data is the ability to exercise real-time high performance data analysis in order to gain insight into the behavior of customers, market trends, business partners, users, etc. Enormous growth in the amount of information businesses must track has greatly challenged legacy database platforms. Current unstructured and text-centric data sources, such as Facebook and Twitter feeds, categorically do not fit into yesterday's "structured" data model. Unstructured data-sets are by definition very big, sloppy and difficult to work with. They require radically new tools and solutions.

Today's businesses require faster insight and profoundly deeper analysis of their data than ever before. Slow performance equals lost income. Hadoop provides a solid answer to this dilemma.

Hadoop is a free, Java-based programming tool for processing massive data sets in a distributed environment. The tool comes from the non-profit

Apache Software Foundation. As shall be delineated later in this report, the powerful but sometimes-unwieldy Hadoop can be brought to heel and made easily manageable by a range of tools, including proprietary Hadoop implementations, offered by major providers catering to the Big Data needs of various enterprises.

An Open Source product, Hadoop has rapidly become the dominant platform for Big Data analytics. Hadoop's principal characteristics are: scalability, flexibility, and economy. Thus it has become vital for enterprises confronted with such issues as extensive click-stream analysis as well as ad targeting. Numerous enterprises who have heretofore been struggling with the limitations of traditional database platforms are now rushing to employ Hadoop in their data analysis scenarios. (These industries are also looking for economy. According to a recent report from Infineta Systems, an impressive start-up concerned with WAN optimization, traditional data storage runs on average $5 per gigabyte, while with Hadoop the storage of identical data costs just 25 cents per gigabyte.)

Hadoop's origins lay in several early implementations, most importantly Google's

MapReduce. The MapReduce program was designed to take an application and break it down into very small parts (sometimes called *fragments* or *blocks*). In turn, any one of these parts can be run on any node in a cluster. Hadoop extends this, empowering enterprises to run applications on systems with literally thousands of nodes embracing thousands of terabytes at one time.

Such a distributed file system (DFS) as this creates very fast data transfer rates amid nodes and empowers the system to continue operating without any perceptible interruption in case of a node failure. Thus the risk of overall catastrophic system failure is negligible even if a large number of nodes fail at once. "The Hadoop platform was designed to solve problems where you have a lot of data — perhaps a mixture of complex and structured data — and it doesn't fit nicely into tables," says Cloudera CEO Mike Olson. "It's for situations where you want to run analytics that are deep and computationally extensive, like clustering and targeting. That's exactly what Google was doing when it was indexing the web and examining user behavior to improve performance algorithms."

The platform is architected to run on a large number of machines - machines that do not memory or disks. Olson: "That means you can buy a whole bunch of commodity servers, slap them in a rack, and run the Hadoop software on each one. When you want to load all of your organization's data into Hadoop, what the software does is bust that data into pieces." Then it spreads all those pieces across your various servers. "There's no one place where you go to talk to all of your data; Hadoop keeps track of where the data resides. And because there are multiple copy stores, data stored on a server that goes offline or dies can be automatically replicated from a known good copy." In the case of a
traditional centralized database, you are working with one large disk usualy linked to from four to
16 robust processors. "But that is as much horsepower as you can bring to bear. In a Hadoop cluster, every one of those servers has two or four or eight CPUs. You can run your indexing job by sending your code to each of the dozens of servers in your cluster, and each server operates on its own little piece of the data. Results are then delivered back to you in a unified whole. That's MapReduce: you map the operation out to all of those servers and then you reduce the results back into a single result set. ... [The] reason you're

able to ask complicated computational questions is because you've got all of these processors, working in parallel, harnessed together."

Hadoop has been deployed by such major players as Google, Yahoo and IBM, largely for applications concerned with targeted advertising and search engines. Although preferred operating systems are Windows and Linux, Hadoop can nevertheless perform well with BSD and OS X. (A bit of trivia: the name *Hadoop* was inspired by the name of a stuffed toy elephant belonging to a child of the framework's creator, Doug Cutting.)

"Facebook uses Hadoop ... extensively to process large data sets," notes Ashish Thusoo, Engineering Manager at Facebook. The firm deploys Hadoop to handle a number of important tasks such as index generation, adhoc analysis, etc. By necessity, Facebook works with one of the world's largest clusters: 23000 cores, 20 PB. The firm also deploys Hadoop (and Scribe) in the process of log collection – to the tune of 50TB of raw data each and every day.

Hadoop is also key to the processing at LinkedIn and Twitter. Hadoop allows both these entities to collect, mine, perform analysis on, and produce highly useful intelligence from data in real-time. "We are excited about the rate of progress that Hadoop is achieving, and will continue our contributions to its thriving Open Source community," notes Kevin Weil, Twitter's Analytics Lead.

Then we have eBay. Back in 2010, eBay built a Hadoop cluster embracing no less than 530 servers. But by December of 2011, that cluster had grown by a factor of five. The firm uses this computing power to do everything from analyzing inventory information to creating profiles of individual customers via study of real-time behavior.

*

Created from work done in Apache by Hortonworks, Yahoo! and other members of the Apache community, the latest Hadoop release incorporates next-generation MapReduce architecture, HDFS Federation and High Availability advancements.

Additional Hadoop-related projects at Apache include: *Avro,* a data serialization system; *Cassandra,* a scalable multi-master database with absolutely no single points of failure; *Chukwa,* a data gathering system for very large distributed systems; *HBase,* a scalable, distributed database supporting the storage of structured data for large tables; *Hive,* a data warehouse incorporating data summarization and supporting ad hoc queries; *Mahout,* a fully scalable machine-learning and data-mining library; *Pig,* a very high-level data-flow language (and execution framework) for parallel processing; and *ZooKeeper,* an elegant, fast coordination service designed specifically for distributed applications.

A Fantastic Kind of Abstraction:

The Origins of HADOOP

We can trace the origins of Hadoop back to 2002. In that year, the Internet Archive's Doug Cutting together with a graduate student (Mike Cafarella from Washington State University) set out to build an open-source search engine they called *Nutch*. This idea was to be able to quickly crawl and process Internet data in what *was then* a great volume: several hundred million web pages. (At this writing, per Ken Kelley of Wired, the Web consists of more than a trillion pages, and is growing at force-10 speed.) In retrospect, Nutch had a number of limitations which were bound to become crippling as the size and rate of data grew. First of all, it could only be run across a few machines at one time. As well, it was so unstable that human-eyes had to be on it 24-7 to make sure it didn't crash.

"I remember being quite proud of what we had been doing ..." notes Cafarella. "[But] then the Google

File System paper came out [October 2003] and I realized: 'Oh, that's a much better way of doing it ...'. Then, by the time we had a first working version, the MapReduce paper came out [December 2004] and that seemed like a pretty good idea too."

Per Mike Olson: Hadoop's underlying technology "was invented by Google back in their earlier days so they could usefully index all the rich textural and structural information they were collecting, and then present meaningful and actionable results to users." Google's paper described a distributed scalable file system for very large, data-intensive, distributed applications. Requiring only highly-economical hardware, the system delivered robust fault-tolerance and very high-aggregate performance across many machines. Of most importance was the scalability: the capability to remain reliable as data grew in volume, and as the number of machines involved increased. At the time the paper was presented, the system was already in use at Google. The firm's largest cluster delivered many hundreds of terabytes of storage on thousands of disks scattered across thousands of machines. The paper was delivered at the 19 ACM Symposium on Operating System Principles held at Lake George, New York in October of 2003. The paper was authored by Sanjay Ghemawat, Howard Gobioff and Shun-Tak Leung.

Authored by Sanjay Ghemawat and Jeffrey Dean, Google's MapReduce paper described an elegant and radically-new programming model together with a superior implementation for creating and processing very large data sets. Within MapReduce, users defined map functions for the process of a key/value pair, this in turn generating a set of key/value pairs together with a reduce function that merged intermediate values merged with the same intermediate key. "Programs written in this functional style are automatically parallelized and executed on a large cluster of commodity machines," wrote the authors. "The run-time system takes care of the details of partitioning the input data, scheduling the program's execution across a set of machines, handling machine failures, and managing the required inter-machine communication. This allows programmers without any experience with parallel and distributed systems to easily utilize the resources of a large distributed system. Our implementation of MapReduce runs on a large cluster of commodity machines and is highly scalable: a typical MapReduce computation processes many terabytes of data on thousands of machines. Programmers find the system easy to use: hundreds of MapReduce programs have been implemented and upwards of one thousand MapReduce jobs are executed on Google's clusters every day."

This paper was presented at OSDI'04: The Sixth Symposium on Operating System Design and Implementation, held in San Francisco in December of 2004.

MapReduce signaled a revolution. Looking back, Raymie Stata, former Yahoo Chief Technology Officer (CTO) and founder of the Hadoop startup VertiCloud, recalls MapReduce as a "fantastic kind of abstraction" over the heretofore common distributed computing procedures and algorithms. "Everyone had something that pretty much was like MapReduce because we were all solving the same problems. We were trying to handle literally billions of web pages on machines that are probably, if you go back and check, epsilon more powerful than today's cell phones. ... So there was no option but to latch hundreds to thousands of machines together to build the index. So it was out of desperation that MapReduce was invented."

The Platform is Born

In the months following the presentation of the MapReduce paper, Cutting and Cafarella began work on the fundamental file systems and framework for processing that would eventually be called *Hadoop*. Importantly, the two pioneers worked using Java even though Google's MapReduce had been implemented using C++. In turn, they layed Nutch across the top of the framework.

Java, they correctly believed, offered the maximum portability they sought in their platform, with its handy "write once, run anywhere" adaptability and its convenient, rich array of class libraries. It should be noted, however, that in recent years some (though by no means *all*) technologists have questioned the wisdom of this move, as an optimized C++ implementation would run just as well while at the same time drawing less hardware capacity and related power. The trade-off, of course, would be ease of portability.

In any event, Hadoop was implemented in Java.

Cutting joined Yahoo as an engineer in 2006, by which time Carfella had become an associate professor at the University of Michigan. It was at this point that Carfella effectively removed himself from commercial Hadoop development in favor of focusing on academics. (He now jokes that his father calls him the "Pete Best'" of Big Data, recalling the original Beatles drummer who was left behind while the band skyrocketed to international fame. Carfella nevertheless continues to work on numerous Hadoop- and Big Data-related projects within the academic setting, and is more than content with his decision.)

At Yahoo, Cutting was charged with building open-source solutions based on the Google File System and MapReduce paradigms. It was at this point that Hadoop (which he'd recently named rather randomly and spontaneously after his young son's toy elephant) became an open-source project with the non-profit Apache Software Foundation. So far as Cutting was concerned, this seemed the ideal approach "because I was looking for more people to work on it, and people who had thousands of computers to run it on."

At this point, Hadoop - although showing great promise - was still quite an inefficient and clumsy implementation, by no means equipped to efficiently handle web-scale search, and Big Data was not yet even seriously envisioned as either a demand or a potential. Hortonworks CEO Eric Baldeschwieler: "The thing you gotta remember is at the time we started adopting it, the aspiration was definitely to rebuild Yahoo's web search infrastructure, but Hadoop only really worked on 5 to 20 nodes at that point, and it wasn't very performant, either."

Today, Raymie Stata talks about the "slow march" towards scalability. In fact, Hadoop development was nothing short of arduous, demanding invention and re-invention over and over again - constantly testing the ingenuity and engineering imagination of all who worked on it. "It was just an ongoing slog ... every factor of 2 or [even] 1.5 ... was serious engineering work."

Very slowly, as the Hadoop technology evolved over the course of several years, Yahoo rolled it out onto what engineers called a "research grid" for use by in-house practitioners of the craft which has since become known as "data science" - the mining of actionable business intelligence from constantly flowing and changing data. At first, Hadoop was engineered to extend across several dozen nodes, then eventually several hundred.

Baldschwieler: "This very quickly kind of exploded and became our core mission, because what happened is the data scientists not only got interesting research results — what we had anticipated — but they also prototyped new applications and demonstrated that those applications could substantially improve Yahoo's search relevance or Yahoo's advertising revenue."

HADOOP Grows Up

Once Hadoop began demonstrating its tangible business viability (round about 2007), a certain level of formality was necessarily adopted around the platform. Yahoo was running most of its business (just about every click/batch process and nearly all the financial transactions) through Hadoop by 2008. Eventually Yahoo used Hadoop for the range of core tasks: hosting line-of-business applications, filtering for spam, and implementing user-specific personalization on individual Yahoo pages. All of this together demanded the creation of service level agreements, not to mention protocols to meet rigid Securities and Exchange Commission requirements with regard to security, seeing how Yahoo began to run all sponsored searches through Hadoop. It also demanded robust and constant growth. By 2011 - in which year Yahoo created its subsidiary firm HortonWorks and spun off all further Hadoop development - Yahoo's Hadoop infrastructure represented no less than 42,000 nodes and many hundreds of petabytes of storage. Concurrent with all this, Hadoop remained a vibrant open-source Apache project, with many individual developers coming up with a vast range of intriguing, robust innovations and solutions.

By far, Yahoo's most valuable contribution to the Hadoop platform was what Yahoo engineers dubbed the "Capacity Scheduler." This tool submits jobs in orderly queues, allocates a portion of resource capacity to each queue, allocates free resources to each queue beyond their total capacity, and assigns and enforces priority labels to the various queues.

Doug Cutting departed Yahoo in August of 2009 to join the start-up Cloudera, which had been founded by Christophe Bisciglia, Mike Olson, Jeff Hammerbacher and Amr Awadallah (the latter a former Yahoo engineering VP) one year earlier. Cloudera represented the very first commercial Hadoop enterprise, and it quickly became the port via which most corporate CIOs got their first look at the platform. Already a favorite of such early adopters as the engineers at Facebook, Hadoop soon became the dominant subject amid the tech industry's constant buzz and chatter. The IT and business press routinely sang the praises of its great promise, this revolutionary approach that offered not only massive economies of scale, but also invaluable real-time BI of a type, quality and timeliness that had not heretofore even been imagined, never mind achieved.

Today the Apache project continues to spur brilliant innovation, while at the same time a number of top software and database firms - among them Amazon, Microsoft and Oracle - offer their own highly-intuitive, emminently-efficient and easy-to-use proprietary commercial variations on the theme. Administering a massive distributed implementation such as Hadoop works with is an extremely complex operation. Most CIOs and corporate IT departments have neither the staff, staff-time or expertise to start from scratch and build a custom Hadoop application and system. Thus a range of vendors have stepped into the marketplace offering robust, easy-to-implement and manage turn-key Hadoop solutions for enterprises that want to get up and running as quickly, economically and safely as possible - without excessive costs and without unnecessary risk to data.

One of the most popular solutions is Amazon's Elastic MapReduce (Amazon EMR). This web service empowers developers, businesses, researchers and data scientists to easily and cost-effectively spin up a custom Hadoop implementation. Amazon EMR is based on a hosted Hadoop framework running on Amazon's robust web-scale infrastructure Amazon Elastic Compute Cloud (Amazon EC2), and utilizes the capacity of Amazon Simple Storage Service (Amazon S3). The combined products allow enterprises to flexibly use as much or as little capacity as they require at any given moment to perform data-intensive tasks related to information mining, web indexing, data warehousing, log file analysis, financial analysis, machine learning, scientific simulation, and other fields of endeavor. Firms using Amazon EMR include razorfish.

Microsoft offers HDInsight, a fully Apache-compatible Hadoop implementation. The product is available for Windows Serever and on Microsoft's Windows Azure platform for Cloud Computing. Oracle's Big Data Applicance incorporates Cloudera's elegant Hadoop implementation, and also includes an implementation of NoSQL, another solution for unstructured data. Other products include Google's Big Query, and a range of offerings from smaller vendors, with more being announced every day.

In the final analysis, Hadoop is here to stay and - in many ways - still in its childhood as a platform.

Much promise remains. Much growth and development is yet to come. The platforms's capacity for increasinly *nuanced* sorting and clearing of huge chunks of unstructured data will only become more robust with the innovation of additional tools and procedures under the Apache umbrella and through R&D at such firms as Yahoo, Amazon and Microsoft. Just as our ability to work with unstructured real-time data has increased in several orders-of-magnitude over the past few years, so it will again in the years to come. It is, in fact, hard at this point to envision what may lay "beyond" Hadoop. It seems itself a frontier, one largely unexplored and under-exploited. So the real question is not what will be next for databases, but what will be next for Hadoop.

More New Street Books and Executive Summaries of Interest

A Simple Introduction to Data Science by Lars Nielsen & Noreen Burlingame

Computing: A Business History by Lars Nielsen

The Little Book of Cloud Computing (Including Coverage of Big Data Tools) by Lars Nielsen

The Little Book of Cloud Computing Security by Lars Nielsen

Low Cost Big Data for Small- to Midsized-Firms and Lean Start-Ups - A New Street Executive Summary by Lars Nielsen

newstreetcommunications.com

Made in the USA
Las Vegas, NV
22 March 2026

44072648R00022